STEEP HOLM
DIARY

Howard and Rosie Smith

The Garret Press

First published in the United Kingdom in November 2006.
The Garret Press, 6 Stafford Place,
Weston-super-Mare, Somerset, BS23 2QZ.
In association with The Kenneth Allsop Memorial Trust.

British Library Cataloguing in Publication Data.
A catalogue record for this book is available
from the British Library.

ISBN 978-0-9541546-6-0
0-9541546-6-5

Cover illustration: Steep Holm from Weston-super-Mare,
October, at sunset.

Design: Colin Baker.

Type: Perpetua

Printed and bound in Great Britain by: R. Booth Limited,
Antron Hill, Mabe, Penryn, Cornwall, TR10 9HH.

STEEP HOLM
DIARY
2001 - 2006

STEEP HOLM - MARCH 2001

In one of his 'island books', Lawrence Durrell describes a condition he calls islomania - "a rare but by no means unknown affliction of the spirit." People so afflicted are irresistibly drawn to islands. And so it is with Steep Holm.

For many in Weston-super-Mare, Steep Holm is a charming piece of rock that slips in and out of the mist on the edge of Weston Bay. Along with its sister island Flat Holm, it occupies a space in the imagination, unattainable, like a remote citadel. But for a group of islomanes, Steep Holm is a place of requited love.

In 1973 the campaigning journalist and naturalist Kenneth Allsop died at the age of 53, and in 1976 a trust, formed in his memory, managed to buy Steep Holm. Its purpose was to conserve the island as a nature reserve. Since then a dedicated band of islomanes have worked at clearing up leftovers from the Second World War, repairing Victorian gun emplacements, monitoring animal and plant life, repairing a blown-up island inn, restoring the Victorian Army barracks and excavating the remains of a mediaeval priory. Regular boat trips arranged during the summer months, visitors cared for and quite a bit else besides. And all for love.

But the island gives an awful lot back. The temperature there is usually a few important degrees warmer than the mainland and, after making the morning sea crossing, there is a special bliss to sitting in the sun above the south facing cliffs.

The sea journey takes about an hour from Knightstone harbour to the pebble beach which faces Weston across the bay. You then follow a zigzag path, past the inn and defunct cottage, and up through a small sycamore wood. Slightly out of breath, you can stop on the cliff path and gaze back across the water to where Weston sits between Worlebury and Brean Down in an unfamiliar perspective. A short climb from there brings you to the top, close to the priory excavations and a Second World War defence battery. Then, with a walk of 300 yards to the west, you arrive outside the Barracks and the splendour of Bridgwater Bay. If you are lucky, and you arrive in early May, the dazzling wild peony *(Paeonia mascula)* will be in flower.

The visiting season runs from April to October but work on the island extends beyond those months. This winter, the island wardens, Jenny Smith and Chris Maslen, have been stoically crossing to and fro in their boat *Skylark*. With the help of a band of volunteers led by Dave Wallace and called 'The Shirkers', scaffolding, for work on the Barracks' roof, has been hauled across to Steep Holm. The roof has been a worry for some years and now the Trust hopes to reslate it during 2001 - given a modicum of good fortune.

Well, it will soon be spring and the *Bristol Queen* will be pushing off from Knightstone again. We shall all be anxious to see how the island has fared over another winter. During the next few months I plan to provide Mercury readers with a monthly diary of the coming and goings on the island, and the stories of a bunch of islomanes.

STEEP HOLM · APRIL 2001

The main problem with a small island in the middle of the Bristol Channel is simply getting there. The rise and fall of the tides are amongst the greatest in the world and severely restrict the opportunities for landing on Steep Holm's small pebble beach. Combine that with gales, storms, fog, and it's not unusual for landings to be impossible for weeks on end. Even for a gang of islomanes.

But despite all these imponderables, the island wardens Chris Maslen and Jenny Smith have got there on their ageing motor vessel *Skylark*. The Victorian Barracks' roof is in desperate need of total repair. To get the work done by a roofing company is way beyond the resources of the Kenneth Allsop Memorial Trust - even if we could find a firm prepared to take the job on! So we shall have to depend on Chris and Jenny and Dave Wallace's cheerful gang called 'The Shirkers'. Most of the wood needed has now been carried across and stored safely. With each trip there is often only 30 minutes or so on the island to unload and carry the wood above the beach (so that it won't be washed away) - the short time enables *Skylark* to head back to Weston with enough sea to reach her mooring at Knightstone.

Approaching the Barracks

In December the paths were given a winter trim, but already the ubiquitous alexanders have made them almost impassable. Alexanders are a sort of Macedonian cow-parsley which were used for the treatment of flatulence (and snake bites) - and they just love growing on Steep Holm! It will be important to clear the paths again during April, before the gulls start to nest. Chris and Jenny have already noted that herring and lesser black-backed gulls are reconnoitring for nesting sites.

As well as taking issue with the Barracks' roof, the winter storms have damaged the quay and washed away the mooring buoy for *Skylark*. With all the comings and goings, the poor boat's 40 year old engine has been under severe strain and had to be 'stripped down'. All this had to be sorted out before any island work could begin.

The early April trip had to be cancelled because of uncertain weather. Also foot and mouth disease has placed restrictions on the island (which has a small family of the tiny Muntjac deer) - this has necessitated disinfectant barriers at the island's gateway. The relative freedom of disease in Somerset and South Wales may afford some protection. The deer are very elusive and shy - it's a big treat to catch sight of one. I never have.

This year the tides are particularly uncooperative - not lining up with weekends etc. - which has meant only one possible visitor trip (already lost) throughout April. The number of potential sailings is down by nearly a third during 2001, although the greater accommodation of the *Bristol Queen* means that we should be able to meet demand.

STEEP HOLM - MAY 2001

With the hard work of transporting the new Barracks' timbers to Steep Holm behind them, it was with relief that Chris and Jenny motored out of Knightstone harbour for the 'long stay'. There was the additional satisfaction of *Skylark* enjoying a new lease of life, having been diagnosed as suffering from 'blocked injectors'. With a reconditioned set, she was now happily burbling across Weston Bay and having no difficulty whatsoever with the race of the tide.

Flat Holm from the northern cliffs

Arriving at the beach, it was straight up to the Victorian Barracks on the the south side of the island where doors were thrown open to allow the spring air into the long room (originally the Army mess) which serves as the trust's visitor centre. Fluttering about inside were butterflies which had woken up from their winter hibernation. In all, Jenny and Chris were able to release eight small tortoiseshell and over twenty peacock butterflies. It is always sad to open up in spring only to find the window-sills scattered with beautiful corpses.

I was up early on Sunday May 6th. The sky was clear and bright, with just the hint of a breeze coming off the estuary. *Bristol Queen* was waiting in the sunshine at Knightstone harbour on the rising tide. By the time I arrived, Joan and Stan Rendell had already sorted out the good-sized crowd of travellers who were busy stowing themselves on board. Even the old hands had a sense of anticipation and excitement for this was the first 'trip' of the season. Steep Holm beckoned in the morning sun on the edge of the bay.

About an hour later we had arrived, making a slow circuit around the island while Stan pointed out various rock formations and Second World War searchlight posts - one involving a descent of 208 steps down a cliff face from which you can watch cormorants nesting and feeding. As we rounded Tower Rock towards the pebble beach, we could see Chris and Jenny waiting to help us disembark. We had to wait a while "for a bit more sea", but within ten minutes or so we were all crunching our way over the beach and then up the zigzag path to the top of the island, a swirl of gulls protesting our arrival.

It was a surprise to find the whole cliff face above the beach brightly decorated with yellow wallflowers, where they have become happily naturalised. At the same time, the island paths were decorated with gulls' nests, for it's now that practically any spare space is bagged by the gulls for nesting purposes - the threat of our passing feet not entering their heads. The nests contain, on average, two to three brown speckled eggs, although Jenny had come upon one with six! Either some sharing was going on or one gull didn't know when to stop. In front of the Barracks, one of the wild peonies was in flower making a brilliant magenta display. This was a rare treat and something I've missed so many times. Sat before the Barracks, in the May sunshine, cup of coffee in hand, this was already a special day.

Wild peony

STEEP HOLM - JUNE 2001

It's been hot and dry on the island for the past six weeks. Very hot at times. Jenny and Chris have had to be careful to avoid dehydration and sunburn. Water has always been a problem for Steep Holm residents. The monks, who lived in the small priory of St. Michael high above the pebble beach, relied on rainwater or collecting the water that trickles from various fissures in the rocks. It's easier for us. Below and behind the Barracks is a 49,000 gallon cistern which collects water from the roof and filters it through pebbles and charcoal. Although not drinkable, this water can be used for cooking, washing and, very importantly, the toilets.

Despite the heat, the heavy work of transporting the slates for the Barracks' new roof across to the island has continued. The good ship *Skylark*, with her new diesel injectors, tirelessly chugging back and forth from Knightstone... five tons so far, only four more to go! Part of the roof scaffolding has been erected - the perfect spot to wave to the paddle-ship *Waverley* as she passed by in the June sunshine. And amongst all this activity, *Bristol Queen* has been bringing visitors once and occasionally twice a week.

The heat has knocked the plant life about a bit and the island is looking a little parched at the moment. The alexanders have flowered, set seed and are now cheerfully ripening well ahead of the game. We can expect a bumper crop next year! Blackberry brambles have been hit by an explosion of lackey moth caterpillars (about two inches long with distinctive blue stripes) leaving the bushes stripped of their leaves. They should quickly recover. Close to the Barracks, Jenny and Chris have set out a vegetable garden and are anticipating a good harvest of runner beans - provided the barrier to keep out the Muntjac deer holds. They've already nobbled the tomato plants.

With help from the Shirkers, our dogged wardens have also been working at clearing the Victorian gun batteries. At Summit Battery, above the Cormorant Cliffs on the north-west side of the island, they came upon a slow-worm at least 51 cm (20 ins) in length. Steep Holm is going for the British record! The gun batteries were constructed in the 1860s; part of a chain across the Bristol Channel to protect us from French invasion.

The semicircular emplacements are beautifully constructed out of Carboniferous limestone - huge blocks, finely worked and finished, fitting closely together. This would have been a difficult enough achievement on the mainland - on this remote island it is staggering. Many of the great guns lie where the Army left them; too hard to cut up: too heavy to carry away.

One day, Chris and Jenny were surprised by two fledgling wrens hopping about on the Barracks' floor, making a great din in the way that hungry young wrens do. Even though they have left the nest, the parents will continue to feed the young birds. And there are no cats on Steep Holm.

Victorian cannon at Summit Battery

Zigzag path through the Sycamore Wood

After describing a parched island last month, a good few
inches of rain promptly fell within a few days and Steep Holm
turned green again. Tramping up through the sycamore wood in
late July, the climate was akin to a tropical rain forest and the
hillside gave off a warm, earthy smell. The sloping woodland
floor was covered with dog and annual mercury, glossy leaves of
hart's tongue fern, and the berried lollipops of lords and ladies
ripening from green to scarlet. Along the edge of the zigzag path
small forget-me-nots were in flower. As I emerged from the
wood onto the top of the island, I noticed that the old buddlia*
above the South Landing was in full bloom. It is now a small tree
and its flowers are a very special bright blue. How it got there
I'm not sure, but it was probably planted around 1974 as a source
of nectar for butterflies. It joins the long list of Steep Holm's
floral curiosities.

Chris and Jenny have erected scaffolding at the eastern end
of the main Barracks building. The decaying 1940's chimney
stack has been taken down and repairs to the gable-end started.
The stone masonry is massive and rather intimidating -
a testament to the Army engineers who built the place back

in the 1860s. But the basic fabric is sound and with a new slate roof should last another 140 years.

At the east end of the island, above the north cliffs, Jenny and Chris have also been tidying up the Laboratory gun battery - so called because it had a lab where gun charges were calculated. With 'Shirkers' Dave Wallace, Ross Willshire and John Jiggins (and me looking on), they were able to move some chunks of huge masonry to reassemble an entrance to the underground magazines. A substantial amount of the original stone from Laboratory Battery was taken by the Royal Engineers in 1940 to construct the island's quay, which had been damaged by recent stormy weather. Blocks of stone have peeled off the quay face so that portions of what was Laboratory battery now lie scattered about the pebble beach. They'll take some getting back - another small job for the Shirkers...

Close to Laboratory battery, clumps of another intriguing plant were growing - the tall yellow spikes of weld *(Reseda luteola)*: an ancient source of a yellow dye. Curiously, weld's flowers are able to follow the sun; in the morning they face east but by late afternoon they will be found looking to the west!

I'm pleased to report that the fledgling wrens, which last month were found protesting on the Barracks' floor, continued to be fed by their parents. After a week or so they flew safely away. Some of the late-hatched young gulls are unlikely to fare so well; their parent birds will probably desert them before they are fully independent. The sight of ill or abandoned birds is always distressing, but in reality there is little that can be done. Steep Holm is a sanctuary for wild life, not a zoo.

This was deliciously misprinted in the Weston Mercury as:
"the old buddha above the South Landing..."

STEEP HOLM · AUGUST 2001

At the end of August, the island has gone quiet. The gulls have departed to their autumn quarters on the mainland and only a few lost or late-hatched youngsters remain - lonely on the shoreline or riding the eddies around the pebble beach.

The uncooperative tides have meant a paucity of possible sailings this summer, but the weather has been kind during August and allowed landings from the Lundy Island ferry *MS Oldenburg* (running weekend Bristol Channel cruises from Clevedon Pier) and *MV Balmoral.* On each occasion, more than 200 passengers were ferried from the big ships by the Weston ferry *Bristol Queen*. The *Bristol Queen* was also kept busy last weekend when Steep Holm received 77 members of the Fortress Study Group. This involved the Weston boat sailing across the Channel to Penarth with Steep Holm vounteers aboard, to pick up the party and transport them to the island. The backwards and forwards business was repeated at the end of the day, with the weary Trust workers staggering off the boat at Knightstone in the late evening after "a marvellous time". Joan and Stan Rendell provided several guided tours, the main source of interest being the Victorian gun batteries and their massive seven inch muzzle loading guns (nine of the original ten remain on the island). Apparently these guns were used throughout the old British Empire and similar defunct artillery still exists in the West Indies and Malta.

Steep Holm has had little rain for over a month and is looking a trifle wrung out once again. The leaves on the sycamore trees hang limply along the bough and impart a rather disconsolate air to the small wood - quite different to their perkiness in moist July. As predicted, the brambles have recovered from the depredations of the Lackey moth caterpillars and the blackberries are starting to ripen. I tasted them from various parts of the island - some sweet and juicy, others sharp and dry. The elders too are heavy with fruit: bunches of black-red berries, glossy and plump. In my garden at home, in Weston, the wood-pigeons feed themselves silly on elderberries and then have upset stomachs -

purple squirts all over the place! But on Steep Holm the berries just hang there, just out of reach of the Muntjac deer - not a passing pigeon to be seen.

The early path clearing by Jenny and Chris has paid great dividends - the routes are wide and clear now, with the bonus of tufty grass under foot. This has made getting around the island easy and comfortable. At the Barracks, the island quiet is broken only by the clink-clink of Mark Smith's masonry hammer as he chips out the old mortar pointing of the Barracks' gables. The roof work is going well and the south side roof timbers have virtually all been replaced and repaired. We hope that this side of the roof will be felted and reslated this year, with the north side following in 2002. It's an heroic task by Chris and Jenny.

STEEP HOLM - OCTOBER 2001

It's really frustrating when the weather forecast turns out wrong. Steep Holm sits out there in the sunshine and I'm stuck on the mainland gazing forlornly across a flat calm sea. And it stays like that all day: the predicted Force 6 - 7 winds never materialising. This year, the last two sailings had to be cancelled (late September and early October) and I felt especially thwarted. Last year at the same time, I had been on the island as the swallows and house-martins were beginning their autumn migration. The weather was warm and balmy. The gulls had decamped, so there was peace and quiet in front of the Barracks where I sat with a mug of Vinah Bell's coffee and a slice of Sue Stops' fruit cake. But then, every half-hour or so, the peace was disturbed by a furious bustle of activity as the island came alive with swallows whizzing at high speed above the brambles and dried out alexanders. And then all would be still.
Until the same extraordinary performance was repeated.
Again and again.

Excavation at the Priory site

I thought at first that the same crowd of swallows and martins were taking a short break before coming back for more insects. But it soon became apparent, and this was confirmed by the island's naturalist Tony Parsons, that each blast of activity was a fresh batch of birds opportunistically dropping in on Steep Holm for a snack on their way south. I suppose the island focused the birds and concentrated their activity into a small space that would normally be taking place over a much wider area.

Chris phoned me from the island to say that this year the martins and swallows had passed through "in their thousands. At times the sky seemed to be speckled with tea leaves." All this went on for two weeks or more - but I still missed it. I shall have to buy a boat.

One of the island's greatest ongoing projects is the archaeological excavation of the ruins of the medieval Priory of St. Michael supervised by Joan and Stan Rendell with the assistance of Terry Gore and Caroline Smith. The priory site is at the top of the island, above the pebble beach, facing Weston. It had been founded during the 12th century and the excavation has shown it must have been a harsh life for the small group of Augustinian canons who lived and died there.

Many of Steep Holm's unusual plants are possible escapes from the priory kitchen garden - for example, the stems and roots of alexanders were eaten during Lent *"...to help digest the crudities and viscious humours which are gathered in the stomach by much use of fish at that time."* But the alexanders may have been waiting for the monks when they landed, brought to the island by the Romans when it was used as a signal station.

Work on the Barracks' roof continues, with reslating almost complete on the south side. Chris and Jenny have also been able to repair the quay wall which had been badly damaged by storm tides. They plan to stay on the island until November, with only the occasional dash to Weston when the seas allow. But for this 'islomane' the sunny spot in front of the Barracks will be unoccupied until March 2002.

STEEP HOLM - MARCH 2002

All week the weather had been slowly improving.
Encouraged, the white blossom on the Shirotae cherry in our
front garden opened, gifting a warm almond scent to the night air.
The moon was filling and, with spring tides higher than 13
metres, a formidable Severn Bore was forecast. The prospects
for the year's first sailing to Steep Holm, on Good Friday,
were looking good.

Arriving at Knightstone just after 8.30am, the *Bristol Queen*
was floating high up against the jetty - just a few steps down from
the causeway. But the Holms, in misty opalescent sunlight, were
nowhere to be seen. In the haze, the promenade had taken on a
mystical Venetian atmosphere, the sea still-calm, grey-green and
metallic. By now, Chris Maslen and Jenny Smith had already been
on Steep Holm for a week and been rewarded with beautiful
weather - if still a little nippy at night. Last year, they had stayed
on the island until early December and had managed to finish
reslating the south side of the Victorian Barracks' roof. During
the winter absence, a chimney pot had blown off and cracked
a few of the new slates - they would have to be replaced before
starting on the 2002 work: the reroofing of the north side.

Having waited for the tide to turn, we eased off from
Knightstone, dawdling past Birnbeck pier while the mainland
started to slide behind frosted glass. At about two miles out,
the Weston shoreline disappeared completely while Steep Holm

remained hidden. We were on our own. But then, as we pushed on into mid-channel, the islands suddenly surprised us, emerging in misty sunlight close by and reassuringly familiar. We made a slow circuit of the island. Gulls circled above the cliffs as cormorants stood sentry on the crags below and shelducks and mallards rested in the sunshine on the lower rocks.

The calm sea made for an effortless landing and Terry Gore, in his high waders, sorted out the idiosyncrasies of the gangplank as usual. Before long, Rosie, Paul Cossham and I were climbing the zigzag path, through the sycamore wood, to the top of the island at Tombstone Battery - so called because 19th century Army masons had placed a memorial slab from the island priory in its walls. From here, the scene was still and breathtakingly beautiful: a smooth and silvery sea, Flat Holm on the edge of visibility, the air tantalisingly spiced with the scent of alexanders. In their various protected places, close to the priory and the Barracks, the Steep Holm wild peonies were accelerating out of the ground, carrying their buds before them. They usually flower in early May. Looks like they might be earlier this year.

And so the day proceeded. Despite his infallible 'internal clock', Paul fell asleep in the sunshine in front of the Barracks and nearly missed the Priory talk. He had to rely on an external nudge from my left foot. We saw a Muntjac deer on one of the pathways (my first ever sighting) and, at the end of the day, two grey seals came to see us all off at the pebble beach. Not bad for the first visit.

Knightstone Island

STEEP HOLM - APRIL 2002

This month, I have been twice thwarted in reaching Steep Holm. First, a strangulated hernia took me into Weston Hospital, followed by a few weeks recuperation while balmy boating days went by. Then, gale force winds, combined with huge spring tides, kept *Bristol Queen* tied up in Knightstone harbour. The seas along the Weston promenade were spectacular, with west winds crashing waves high over the sea-wall. Not the sort of weather to be out in. Indeed, the storm was an echo of the 1990 tempest which plucked an earlier Steep Holm ferry *Weston Lady* from the slipway at Knightstone and deposited her, in fragments, along the esplanade. Stan and Joan Rendell, in their book *Steep Holm,* recount this last voyage along the wrong side of the sea-wall. Amazed hotel guests watched as the poor *Lady* sailed by on the flooded promenade, ending up in bits opposite the Royal Hotel lawns.

Meanwhile, the island's intrepid wardens, Chris and Jenny, were out in it all "keeping our heads down." From their island fastness, they watched enormous seas and massive standing waves smash into Rudder Rock, Steep Holm's western tip. They were pleased to report that quay repairs at the pebble beach had withstood this latest challenge, and the Barracks' roof was still intact. Although this end of April had been a trifle vivid, the rest of the month had been kind with sunny, breezy days. The wind had made further roof work difficult, but the scaffolding has been repositioned in preparation for the next phase on the north side.

As I feared a few weeks ago, Chris tells me the peonies are already flowering - two weeks early. The flowers last a few weeks at most but are truly splendid. Bright carmine, single flowers are held well above their luxuriant leaves. They were possibly introduced by the island's priory monks for medical use, although I haven't been able to find out what. Strangulated hernias perhaps. The plant puts on a second show later in the year with big pods containing red and black seeds. The island trust sells the seeds, as well as small plants germinated on the mainland.

Rudder Rock

Jenny and Chris report that the island is busy with butterflies. They've seen holly blues, green veined whites, small tortoiseshells, peacocks and even the odd red admiral. Holly blues are interesting butterflies in that their caterpillars are not picky in their choice of food plant. They like holly buds and then ivy later in the year, but will settle for gorse or bramble if needs must! It explains why they do well on Steep Holm.

Sad to relate that two Muntjac deer have been found dead, apparently from falls. The gulls have laid their eggs and are becoming vociferous and protective. Sparrowhawks have been seen disturbing the roosting gulls with low inquisitive flights.

Small tortoiseshell

STEEP HOLM · JUNE 2002

After a wet and windy few days, the weather decided to behave itself and we were able to set sail for Steep Holm on a mid-morning tide. As we approached the island, the cliff tops above Tower Rock had a light blush about them. Tree mallow was in full and exultant flower, enjoying one of the years when it takes over the southern cliffs. The plants lined the first part of the zigzag path up from the beach - in their two years of existence (they're biennials) they grow shoulder high (even up to nine feet) with multiple stalks of purple-pink hollyhock flowers. They do well by the sea and, like so many of Steep Holm's plants, have a medicinal function; they can be made into ointments, poultices or infusions to soothe muscle pain. Useful after going up and down the zigzag path a few times. The tree mallow is a native plant, though considered rare outside the south-west.

The Barracks' Terrace

But, for all the success of the tree mallows, members of the Rose genus were having a hard time of it. Contrary to expectations, blue-striped lackey moth caterpillars have achieved plague-like proportions for a second year running, and they just love the Rose family! On the warmer south side of the island, the blackberries have been stripped of their leaves, and whitebeam trees, which should have been in full leaf, were bare-branched

against the sky. The caterpillars
even nobbled Jenny's potted
strawberry plants, dropping onto
them, commando style, from
scaffolding close to the
Barracks' garden. They seem
predisposed to climb forever
upwards, scaling walls,
windows and, especially,
scaffolding poles. They march,
with military determination,
to the top of the poles which
they cap with a woolly hat of
squirming caterpillars.

Tree mallow

As before, the shrubs and trees should
recover, but they will have lost a lot of this year's growth. Why
this pestilence has been visited upon Steep Holm for a second year
isn't clear. It's possibly a failure of their natural predators, such as
the small wasps whose larvae, rather gruesomely, eat the
caterpillars from the inside. Perhaps the little blighters will eat
themselves out of hearth and home, starve themselves to death,
and get back to reasonable numbers once again.

Although it was cool when we set off from Knightstone,
on the terrace outside the Barracks it was sheltered and warm.
Scrumptious home-made, chocolate-date cake (courtesy of Pam
Wallace) fitted very well with a cup of coffee, as I sat looking
out over Bridgwater Bay, the coastline arcing from Brean Down
to Porlock Weir. A pair of herring gulls were also pretty
comfortable; they had a nest parked in the Barracks' herb garden
with two nestlings, not long hatched. The parent birds stood on
the Barracks' Georgian cannon, nattering and complaining.
Then, every now and again, they made a dash across the terrace
to check and feed their young. All in all, they seemed to have
accepted human intrusion. The frequent comings and goings
of Chris and Jenny had seen to that.

STEEP HOLM - JULY 2002

From where I'm sitting, on the terrace in front of the island Barracks, the gulls rise and slide in the wind. They fall out of sight below the escarpment only to re-emerge tilting into the breeze or shooting straight upwards, as though they had been shot from guns. All this is accompanied by cries and screeching, airborne posturing to defend an invisible volume of air. Passing birds are worked over, the dogfight tumbling away in a series of stall turns.

This especially aggressive behaviour seems to be acquired at hatching. The young gulls, which were mere balls of fluff nesting in the Barracks' garden when I was last here four weeks ago, are now like an adolescent street gang patrolling the grass in front of the terrace. Now and again a chick (who was misguidedly reared up on the Barracks' roof and then fell off) strays into gangland territory and gets beaten up. From its perch on top of the Georgian cannon, a parent bird watches with an approving, yellow eye.

Rain has kept the island green and the plague of lackey moth caterpillars has passed. Already the whitebeams are in fresh grey-green leaf, spring-like after the depredations of the caterpillars. The brambles too are releafing themselves at high speed. The caterpillars have left tents of tough silky webs which are filled with their cast-off skins (and heads). These tents are now occupied by earwig families feeding on the redundant epidermis. Each to its own.

The archaeological dig at the medieval priory site is always difficult during gull nesting time. Not unreasonably, the birds ind the grassy earthworks very comfortable for raising a family; so Joan, Stan and Terry spend much of the early summer tidying up and preparing for the birds' departure. The nests are now empty, so the dig can proceed. Last year, the team felt that the investigation of the little church's foundations was coming to an end when, suddenly, a thick stone wall surfaced in an unexpected place - almost in the centre of the priory. It was in the wrong position to support a tower, in fact it was in the wrong position for anything! So a lot more earth has to be shifted and sifted over the next few months. "Not quite 'Time Team' stuff." says Stan. But it's an intriguing little mystery all the same.

The Inn and Cliff Cottage

Earlier in the day, as we rounded Tower Rock on our landing approach, Tony Parsons pointed out four small brown birds moving up and down the rocks above the tide line. They were common sandpipers and not often seen on Steep Holm. Tony speculated that they were probably on their way south to Africa, having nested in Scandinavia. Later in the afternoon Tony showed me a glass tube containing turnip beetles - small black bugs with yellow stripes which feed on the island's wild turnips. Their other name is striped flea beetles because they jump like fleas when disturbed. But don't worry - they only bite turnips!

STEEP HOLM · AUGUST 2002

A couple of times in each summer season, Steep Holm launches itself into a day of furious activity. The *Bristol Queen* sets off from Knightstone harbour in the usual way, but on these occasions there are no trippers aboard. The island volunteers make the journey alone, although they won't be lonely for long. As the boat drives into the pebble beach, Chris and Jenny are waiting. Those with secure arms and lumbar spines stay on the beach while the rest hurry up the zigzag path to the Barracks' Visitor Centre.

In the Barracks, last minute preparations are made. The counter dust-covers are lifted and books, island stamps, peony seeds, postcards and souvenirs displayed. Kettles are filled and set down on the kitchen stoves. Home-made cakes sliced. Then the call goes out "She's here!" We all rush out onto the terrace and look down upon the graceful lines of the *MV Balmoral*. We wave and the beautiful boat rattles her anchors in reply, while we try to guess how many people are on board. She looks pretty crowded, and there'll be even more adventurers queuing unseen below deck - they will be the first off. Today, the travellers will have embarked at harbours in Bristol, Portishead or Penarth (all 249 of them), but on other sailings people have come from Clevedon and even Minehead.

Bristol Queen, which has been waiting in the wings of this drama, now enters stage left and starts to ferry visitors from the big boat to the beach - this is where the safe backs and hands are needed. It takes about half an hour to get everyone safely onto the island and about another 15 minutes or so before they begin to arrive, hot and a bit short of puff, at the Barracks. A few have been to

Steep Holm before and are keen to see if anything has changed. Some, like all of us in the Kenneth Allsop Trust (islomanes to a man), are drawn by the mystery and beauty of the place. Others may have heard about Pam Wallace's chocolate-date cake.

Our guests spend more than five hours on the island and keep us fully occupied with questions about 'life on Steep Holm': the birds, animals and plants, and "How do the wardens survive?!" The mainland coast provides a fascinating and, for a few, a disorienting backcloth to the day. Some say Weston and Brean Down don't look the same somehow, and confuse the Quantock hills for Wales.

Too soon, they have to return to the beach, the ferry and then *Balmoral*, for their various journeys home. For the volunteers there is little respite; the Barracks are speedily tidied up and then it's back to Knightstone on the evening tide. There are only a few hours left to prepare for the 'ordinary' island sailing the next day - and the *Bristol Queen* is booked to capacity. And people ask why we can't have more trips!

On the morning of the *Balmoral* visit, the main roof of the Barracks received its final ridge tile completing the 18 months of hard labour carried out by Chris and Jenny. Waterproof at last. Tremendous! Now for the eastern block…

(This piece was co-written with Joan Rendell)

Home-made cakes!

STEEP HOLM - SEPTEMBER 2002

A few evenings ago, Chris phoned to say that he and Jenny would be doing a daytime round trip on their boat *Skylark*. They planned to get more roofing materials onto the island and would I like to accompany them? Would I! For some time, I had been angling for a trip on *Skylark* and, at last, weather and tides were co-operating to make it possible.

I arrived at Knightstone just before nine, on one of those magical mornings - a clear blue sky, little wind and the sea flat calm. Waiting for *Skylark* to be brought to the quayside, the curve of the high harbour wall seemed to focus the sun's early warmth. A scatter of people peered over with benign curiosity as I helped load water bottles which Joan and Stan Rendell had brought for the Saturday trip the next day. Tomorrow, the ferry *Bristol Queen* would carry nearly ninety visitors to the island, but today I was going to have Steep Holm to myself. Well almost.

We set off from Knightstone just before 10 o'clock - about three hours after high water. This meant the tide, which was beating its twice daily retreat from Weston, would carry us out into mid-channel at about four miles an hour - that would save *Skylark's* old diesel engine, reduce fuel and speed the journey. We made good time to the island, arriving with the sea still a little too high on the pebble beach - so we coasted around to the south side, now basking in late summer sunshine. Suddenly, there was a disturbance amongst the gulls. Jenny pointed out a sparrow-hawk skimming above the shrubs covering the southern cliffs. Gulls were unlikely to be on the hawk's menu - too big for the oven. It would be the small birds, like dunnocks or wrens, which would fall prey.

At the beach, Chris drove *Skylark* hard onto the pebbles and we waited awhile for the tide to leave us, neatly stranded, tilting to starboard. This made it possible to unload the boat in our own time - the sea wouldn't be back until after six that evening. About an hour after landing, roofing felt and heavy (very) rolls of lead flashing were delivered to the Barracks for the final phase of roofing work on its small eastern block. The weather then surprised us with a short but unreasonable squall of sharp rain which promptly vanished into the dry soil. Mid-afternoon, I took up some secateurs and meandered the island's pathways, snipping back the brambles which could throw a thorny arm across a track in a few days. As I was busy at the Split Rock Battery magazine, the sparrowhawk we had seen earlier took off from the entrance and flew at speed over the crest of the island.

Beaching Skylark

By 6.30 that evening, the sea was picking at *Skylark's* stern and within a few minutes of boarding we were fully afloat, using the incoming tide to carry us back to Weston. Back at Knightstone, I watched from the promenade as Jenny and Chris moored *Skylark* and then boarded their inflatable which would take them straight back to Steep Holm. This time against the tide.

The island is always surprising us. Plants can go missing for years and then arrange an unexpected reappearance. The latest example of this is the engagingly named white ramping fumitory which has sprung up by the old farmhouse ruin, at the eastern end of the island, close to the medieval priory. Actually it's not ramping quite so much these days - indeed it has become very rare. It is an attractive plant with small cream flowers that have reddish tips. Its leaves are bright green and ferny - a bit like flat leafed parsley. Apparently, if fumitories are pulled up, they release a gaseous fume (hence their name) which smells of nitric acid! We shan't be trying that.

White Ramping fumitory

According to Tony Parsons, the white ramping fumitory was last recorded on Steep Holm in 1910, and you might just wonder what it's been doing over the past 92 years. Seed can lie dormant until woken up by some disturbance. An example of this is the blaze of red poppies which spring up on building sites or along new road workings. Jenny and Chris had been helping to dig a new pond and had stirred up the old fumitory seed. So perhaps it will get ramping once again.

Close by the pond, cut-leaved cranesbill appeared (a relative of the wild geranium herb robert) which is common enough on the mainland but was last noted on the island by a group of naturalists in 1883! On top of all this, to the south, close to the Barracks, yellow-wort has popped up in two places. This is a slender, yellow flowered plant, fairly common on limestone grassland, which hasn't been seen for 79 years. Tony has also noted a completely new plant to Steep Holm: the dwarf mallow - a close relative of the tree mallows whose lilac flowers were so abundant in May and June, covering the sunnier slopes of the island. Now where did that come from?! But perhaps it's been there all along, skulking about Split Rock.

A few weeks ago, Steep Holm suffered a cool, wet day (I wasn't there, so I don't believe it). To cheer up the visitors, who were intermittently confined to barracks, it was decided to light a fire. As a log was being lowered into the flames a lesser stag beetle *(Dorcus parallelipipedus)* staggered out. The log had been gathered from the island's beach, so the beetle had already made an intrepid journey from the mainland; possibly all the way down the Wye or the far reaches of the Severn. It almost goes without saying this was the first record of a lesser stag beetle on the island! So it's going to be a bit lonely and it doesn't have much time; the adult beetle only lives for a month or so. But perhaps it knows something that Tony Parsons doesn't.

Lesser stag beetle

While I was last there in late September, it was warm and sunny, although the air had an autumnal twitch to it. Once again, the island was alive with swallows and martins dropping in to feed before continuing their long migration south. Our old pal the grey seal looked in at the pebble beach and we spent a good while staring at one another. One more visit perhaps, then it's good-bye until next spring.

Swallows

STEEP HOLM · MARCH 2003

My hopes of a closing visit to the island last October were thwarted by high winds. Jenny and Chris, however, stayed on Steep Holm until mid-December. Having completed the huge task of re-roofing the Victorian Barracks during 2002, they had got well ahead with work on the East Block before winter closed them down. Slates are now in place within a row or two of the ridge, so another important building should be weatherproof and dry within the next month or so. The logistics of any building work on the island are daunting. Just getting the materials (usually very heavy) across the water means snatching moments when the weather and tides are favourable, combined with the strength to haul the stuff ashore. The good ship *Skylark* has made 15 round trips so far, and what Chris and Jenny have achieved is well beyond the call of duty - the Kenneth Allsop Trust is hugely grateful for their efforts.

Winter is a pretty hostile time on the island and visits there are unusual, being normally linked to a special purpose. My only experience (and Rosie's too) was in December 1989. Rodney Legg, the island's warden at that time, had lined up a gang of Trust members to plant trees (mainly whitebeams) in various areas above the southern perimeter path. It was bitterly cold, though planting trees, into what seemed like solid rock, generated a fair amount of warmth! Lunch was spent huddled around a driftwood fire in the Barracks - quite romantic really - in an effort to get fingers and toes back into the land of sensation. Rosie reckons she has never been so cold in all her life - and that includes the time we survived an Albertan winter with temperatures of 40 degrees below zero. When we got back to Weston, we warmed up over a pizza at Pescara's (now Tarantella's) in St. James Street. Never has a pizza tasted so good! And the trees? Well, to my amazement the planting was a success and a fair number have become established - they were in good leaf last summer, 13 years later, and that's despite the eating habits of the lackey moth caterpillar (see June 2002).

Sometimes the island seems to have an inspirational effect. In August last year, a group of firemen from the Bristol Fire Brigade (Steep Holm lies within the administration of the Port of Bristol) elected to lend the Trust a replacement fire pump. On December 7th, a team of Royal Navy Volunteer Reservists, complete with the pump, arrived off Steep Holm in the ex-Navy boat *Pride of Bristol.* The weather was grey and windy; the sea at the pebble beach too rough to land. The Navy was not to be deterred. The boat stood off until low water, when it was possible to get ashore with the pebble spit acting as a breakwater. The heavy pump was unloaded and carried by the Reservists to the top of the island. After a brief rest for refreshment, the team had to return to the *Pride of Bristol,* but by then the tide had turned and it was too dangerous to attempt embarkation from the beach. Luckily the island has a southern World War II jetty (a trifle worn) where, in gathering darkness, the boarding succeeded. The ship and crew then parked themselves in the lee of the island for the night, with further adventures planned for the next day.

The beach at South Landing

STEEP HOLM - APRIL 2003

Chris telephoned to say that he and Jenny were "crossing over to the island with a ton of bricks on the *Skylark* in a few days time." Did I fancy a trip? I hadn't been to Steep Holm so early in the season and with all the sunny weather it seemed an ideal opportunity. Except for the ton of bricks.

The weather was perfect. Warm and still. At 10.15, when I arrived at Knightstone, the bricks were already aboard. The delivery lorry had managed to lower them into *Skylark* by crane from the slipway - that saved a lot of time and sweat. The previous day had seen one of the highest spring tides of the year - more than 14 metres - which, at its height, had lapped only a few feet below the top of the sea-wall. Sitting in *Skylark*, I could see where the tide had reached, for the mark was way above me with the sea falling rapidly.

Chris unloading Skylark

Weston had on her Venetian clothes with a pale sun, a thin mistiness cloaking the town and the sea flat calm. We waited awhile for the sea to fall a little further and then set out on our tide-assisted passage. By now, Steep Holm was just visible.

Knowing it was there, I could make out its ghosty shape just where the sea disappeared into the mist - it would be a while yet before Flat Holm cast off her shroud. We chugged out across placid water - just a hint of disturbance as we passed over the shallows of the 'Weston Ledge', a mile or so out from Anchor Head. We were travelling at a good four to five knots in a smooth sea. Half way across, a large dark shape, low in the water, sailed into view. It was a huge tree trunk travelling at some speed in the tidal race. It would have been invisible at night - easy to imagine the damage it could inflict. Indeed, scanning the surface showed up several more displaced trees cruising on a south-west course; the very high tides had scooped them up from their seashore moorings. Where they would end up was anyone's guess.

When we reached Steep Holm, the tide was still too high for a safe landing on the pebble beach. So we made a slow circuit of the island. The gulls were back; our course anticipated by their loud squalling and complaining cries. Cormorants flew dark and low over the water or stood observing us from their fastness on the northern cliffs. A group of shelduck, in their black and white tuxedos, took off from below Tower Rock.

At last the sea was just right. Chris drove *Skylark* onto the beach and, as the tide retreated, she leaned, comfortably stranded, over to one side. From here, we unloaded the bricks onto the island's beloved Honda Load-carrier* and then up the pebbled slope to the jetty. Next, the bricks had to be winched 18 ft to the top of the quay wall where they were unloaded to await the final journey to the top of the island. To get the ton of bricks into position at Laboratory Battery (whose underground magazine brickwork needs repair) took many separate journeys with multiple loadings and unloadings in-between.

Meanwhile, the gulls are taking up nesting positions, the wild peonies are breaking cover, the whitebeams making grey-green leaf and the Barracks' roof has survived the winter repair work intact. Chris's Steep Holm Ale tasted pretty good too.

A motorised 'wheel-barrow' with caterpillar tracks.

STEEP HOLM - MAY 2003

We're having a frustrating time. Our ferry boat *Bristol Queen* has had fitting and servicing delays so the early season trips to Steep Holm have had to be cancelled. Especially annoying when all April the sun was shining down. Even more so, since I've once again missed the flowering of the wild peony. There is a precious window of ten days or so, usually in the first few weeks of May, when it puts on its scarlet show. Chris says the warm April weather had brought everything forward by several weeks - so the peonies had performed and drawn the final curtain by Easter. And that's it. Gone for another year. I can't stand it.

The extraordinary dry sunny weather we have all enjoyed for the seven weeks up to Easter, broke with high tides and high winds on the island. Easterly gales pushed the sea over the quay at the pebble beach. Waves broke over the boathouse and the metal gangplank, used to disembark visitors from *Bristol Queen*, was almost washed away. On one of the very low tides (which accompany the high spring tides) Chris and Jenny were able to explore areas of the shore normally inaccessible or under water. They came upon a rusty coloured edible crab *(Carcinus pagurus)*. At four inches across the shell (they can reach eight inches), not quite big enough to grace their table, but large for these here parts. They are more common on the south coast. Indeed, this was the first time either Jenny or Chris had seen an edible crab on Steep Holm. The ones they usually come across, and which children catch at Anchor Head jetty, are the small green shore crabs *(Carcinus maenas)*. The British don't eat the shore crab although they do on the Continent. Which, I'm sure, suits the shore crab very well and they must be fairly smug about not being called 'edible' either.

Rosie and I have been exploring the West Somerset coastline over the past year. Steep Holm is always in view, changing shape as you move westwards. Gone is Weston's currant bun perspective, and indeed the island looks quite uninviting; all you can see are the steep southern cliffs. Chris tells me the alexanders are in full rampant bloom at the moment and we've noticed that all along the Somerset shore, and also quite a way inland, the alexanders are luxuriating. It must be an indicator of global warming for such a Mediterranean plant to be doing so well. Smelling their sweet, spicy scent always reminds me of Steep Holm and I have a suspicion Somerset's coastal colonies started from there.

Tony Parsons swathed in Alexanders

Greenfinches and goldcrests have passed through the island. The sparrowhawk I reported on last year has been upsetting the gulls again. It has a favourite pastime of flying close to the cliffs, sending the gulls screaming with alarm from one end of the island to the other. "It's like a Mexican wave." says Chris. They counted 17 crows in the sycamore wood - behaving disgracefully, as always. Swallows dropped by on their return from Africa. They'll be seen again when they pass through on their winter migration. Since mid-April, butterflies have been on the increase. Jenny has noted holly blues, green-veined and small whites, orange tips and painted ladies. This morning I cycled past Birnbeck, high up on the Kewstoke Road. It was cold and drizzly, but Steep Holm had arranged a pocket of sunshine to sit in… Come on *Bristol Queen*!

STEEP HOLM - JUNE 2003

After her trials and tribulations, it was good to find
Bristol Queen waiting by the jetty at Knightstone Harbour.
The increasing burden of regulation is making it difficult for the
small boatman to survive and it's a main reason why Weston now
has so few. It was good too, to have a 60 strong crowd of visitors
prepared to brave the Severn Sea at 9.30 in the morning.

We set off, beating into a cool north-west wind, but the thin
high cloud promised a sunny day. The journey across was
uneventful until we reached Steep Holm's pebble beach.
Here, the tide race was unexpectedly strong: the sea accelerating
over the shingle spit and churning below Tower Rock. Long ago,
the shingle spit was lined with wooden stakes hung with nets and
baskets to catch salmon - a fresh attempt in the 1930s didn't pay
and hasn't been tried since. What salmon there might be these
days are left to our resident grey seals.

Meanwhile, *Bristol Queen* backed off, waited awhile for the
current to abate and made an uncomplicated landing with everyone
on the beach and not a single wet foot - except for Terry Gore that
is. His high rubber waders, as always, filled up with sea water
which he uncomplainingly accepted as he helped people down the
gangway. With everyone ashore, *Bristol Queen* pulled away and
disappeared around Tower Rock, leaving me with that delicious
feeling of isolation I always have whenever I come to Steep Holm.

As ever, the gulls were in noisy evidence; their breeding
period well advanced with many nests occupied by two or three
fluffy brown nestlings. Last year, the cliffs had been covered with
the violet blush of flowering tree mallow. This year, there was
little of this sea-cliff plant to be seen - just a small cluster at the
base of the eastern cliffs that face Weston. The island was dotted
with white, flat elder flowers - a good two weeks ahead of the
mainland and their scent, combined with the alexanders, made
the place smell like a spice emporium. Another plant I noticed
was hound's-tongue (I didn't actually know it was hound's-tongue;
Jenny so advised). This too was growing close to the eastern cliffs

and is a tall, upright plant with dark red flowers. It belongs to the forget-me-not family and its leaves were once used to treat the bite of a mad dog!

In the late morning I was alerted that a peregrine falcon had been spotted flying amongst the gulls below the north cliffs. When I got there, I found myself, uniquely, looking down on the broad powerful wings of the bird. The peregrine appeared to be strolling above the sea in slow, languid loops and not especially interested in anything except upsetting the gulls. The peregrine falcon has been the island's figurehead since the founding of the Kenneth Allsop Trust. For many years the bird approached extinction due to the use of the insecticide DDT but is now back to healthy numbers. These days there is often a breeding pair in an eyrie on the cliffs.

We had some entertainment testing the fire hoses donated to us by the Avon Fire Brigade. It was a bit like a 'Keystone Kops' movie round the back of the Barracks, rolling out hose with no end in sight. I expected there to be the sort of squirting leaks you get in 'The Beano' and was, frankly, disappointed when it all worked perfectly!

Disembarking from Bristol Queen

STEEP HOLM - JULY 2003

After a blistering weekend, the forecast for my trip to the island was mixed. Two days earlier, the blazing sun had had the Steep Holm visitors seeking shade wherever they could find it, and few had managed to stagger round the island more than once. It was just too hot. Even the gulls were stunned into a semblance of silence.

The dry, warm June has taken its toll and many fledgling gulls have succumbed to the drought. It's always distressing to come upon a sick or injured youngster and, at this time of year, their corpses line the pebble beach at the bottom of the eastern cliffs. You can often make them out in the sea, struggling to get back into the air, having landed in the water during an early attempt at flight. Despite the high mortality, gull numbers are rising. They are even moving into the urban settings of Bristol and Bath, where their aggressive behaviour is making them increasingly unpopular.

Extreme low tide on the Shingle Spit

Today it was overcast as we set off from Knightstone, and the Holms were a murky presence mid-channel. There had been quite a bit of rain the night before - the first for some time - and now a fine drizzle accompanied us on our journey with rather more passengers resorting to *Bristol Queens*' cabin for coffee than usual. Amazingly (as is so often the case on Steep Holm), by the time we landed, the clouds were breaking up and the temperature was rising. The summer rain had given the sycamore wood a bosky smell and the trees did not look as distressed as I expected. The interminable rains of May had laid down plenty of water in the bedrock, although the rest of the island looked pretty parched. Chris told me the Muntjac deer were even coming down to the Barracks for water. With Jenny and Chris's continuous presence on the island, the deer are becoming much bolder and sightings are far more frequent these days.

One of the jobs I had to do on this visit was help Chris measure the gradient of the pebble beach. Martin Wools, *Bristol Queens*' skipper, has been considering obtaining a small, front-loading, ferry. This would make it much easier and faster to embark and disembark onto the beach. At Knightstone, it might be possible to use the wide slipway - also an attractive prospect. Anyway, with a spirit level and a touch of Pythagorus, Chris and I worked out the beach gradient, in the landing zone, to be 1 : 5. Higher up the beach, it was 1 : 4. Pebble movement across the beach is enormous and its appearance is constantly changing. After a storm, the pebbles can be piled up against the cliffs, covering rocks normally quite a feature of the scene. For the first time, I realised that a lot of the massive stones at the northern end of the beach were the remains of a small pre-Victorian harbour. When the inn was built around 1830, a harbour pier was also constructed. A watercolour painting of 1858 shows the walls still standing but, within another 20 years, it had all but disappeared.

STEEP HOLM - AUGUST 2003

The Severn Sea is a perverse stretch of water. After weeks of kindly weather, we seemed well set to greet the 300 passengers from the *MV Balmoral* when she made her annual visit to Steep Holm. This time, the visitors were to spend six hours on the island (rather longer than usual) so we had to bring in extra supplies and volunteer help. *Balmoral* was due to arrive at 1pm and, encouragingly, our ferryboat *Bristol Queen* had already made a 'Trip around the Bay', earlier that morning with smooth, calm water.

Since she was staying with us for the week, I invited my niece Harriet (who now lives in France) and her boyfriend Jerome to come for the trip. Harriet has sunny memories of Steep Holm from a time she visited the island, eleven years ago, when she was five. When we arrived at Knightstone quay, it was overcast with a slight flick of rain. But in the west it was reassuring; the cloud was breaking up and there was sunshine along the Welsh coast. However, the calm waters of the early morning had given way to 'a bit of sea' and there was full westerly breeze of Force 4 - 5 to contend with. *Bristol Queen* is a good-sized boat and the waves we met beyond the Knightstone pier were no problem for her - although they did succeed in filling my right shoe. Our concern now was the choppy sea might make it difficult to land the *Balmoral* passengers onto Steep Holm, which was to involve *Bristol Queen* transferring about 90 people at a time from the big boat and bringing them to the island's pebble beach.

Except for my wet foot, we arrived and landed without incident. I stayed on the beach with Terry Gore and Dave Wallace to help the mass disembarkation, while Harriet and the others pressed on up to the Barracks to make ready. Suddenly *Balmoral* was there, only to disappear to the more sheltered southern lee of the island. Time went by... 15 minutes... 25 minutes... neither sight nor sound. I decided to go up to the island top, to find out what was going on. From high up, I could see the two boats, stationary, 60 yards apart, in what appeared to be calm water. Another 20 minutes went by. I knew that time was running out since the tide was already falling when I had left the beach. Soon there wouldn't be enough sea for *Bristol Queen* to land one, let alone four boatloads of visitors from *Balmoral*. Eventually, with a few desultory waving arms, the two boats pulled away, leaving us alone, in the sunshine, on the island.

MV Balmoral from the Barracks' terrace

We later found out *Balmoral* had been dragging her anchor, presumably due to a strong crosscurrent, and had been unable to remain still enough to allow her passengers board *Bristol Queen*. It must have been so frustrating for those people to be so close to the island and unable to land. And we must have looked tiresomely idyllic, standing before the Barracks, waving to them in the sunshine! Harriet and Jerome had a good day though - with Steep Holm virtually to themselves. At about 6 o'clock, I caught sight of the *Balmoral* slowing down and making a wistful pass, a short way off the pebble beach. Well, maybe next year.

STEEP HOLM - SEPTEMBER 2003

There was a definite suggestion of Autumn on the air, as just under ninety of us gathered at Knightstone harbour on a late-September morning. The forecast was good and the sun was already showing on Birnbeck. We moved out on a falling 13 metre tide which meant the tide-race at the island was likely to be brisk. My friends Andrew and Joy Wilson had been out to Steep Holm for the first time earlier in the year and had fallen in love with the place. It would appear they are now *islomanes.* I hoped the island would deliver the goods a second time.

The tidal race was indeed energetic and *Bristol Queen* had to stand off for a while but the landing went smoothly. When I got to the Barracks, the buddleia, tucked in by one of the doors, was covered in an assortment of fluttering butterflies. There were painted ladies, small tortoiseshells (the large tortoiseshell is now very rare in Great Britain) and large whites. The occasional red admiral dropped in for a feed too. It's been a good year for butterflies on Steep Holm; Jenny has reported seeing a pair of clouded yellows, migrants from southern Europe, which are relatively rare.

Inside the Barracks, Stan Rendell was sorting out peony seeds. The seed-capsules make a vivid display of red and black seeds. But only the black jobs are fertile. The Kenneth Allsop Trust sells them, five at a time. They are slow to germinate - putting them in the fridge helps - but it is a way of maintaining the plant. Being at the edge of their range, the peonies on the island are always under some threat, through climate or disease.

I met up with Tony Parsons at the top of the island where Chris and Jenny have been working at extending the area of grassland. Once again, I became aware of my ornithological blindness. I don't see birds. But while I was with Tony: four ravens arrived high above us, hung about for a while, and then flew off in separate directions (ravens breed on the island and have been known to take gull chicks); a skylark hovered in the air before dropping back to ground, and swallows and house martins flew low about us, calling in at Steep Holm on their migration south.

Back at the Barracks, Joy and Andrew were sitting contentedly on the terrace gazing out over a sun-dappled sea towards the West Somerset coast. It was seriously idyllic. Steep Holm was putting on a very good show. Just as well, for one of the present visitors had come last year when it had pelted down all day. But he still came back.

I now left to view John Jiggins' pond. He was a bit fed up because he had hit bedrock, but the pond looked pretty deep to me. He was also disconcerted when I pointed out an odd piece of stone with HVN carved into it - although it could have been NAH, if you held it up the other way. Anyway it was 'Very Interesting' and I pointed out to John that he might have disturbed an Important Archaeological Site and would have to fill his pond back up. Stan said it was a lump of concrete from WW2. But I wasn't convinced...

Bristol Queen collected us as the sun lowered over the top of the island. We sailed back in a dazzle of golden light. It was all too good to be true, but Andrew has the photographs to prove it was real.

Leaving Steep Holm

STEEP HOLM · DECEMBER 2003

The dry weather continued through Autumn into the first week of November when the much-needed rain at last arrived. By early October the *Bristol Queen* had taken and returned the last boatload of visitors to Steep Holm. All in all it had been a good season with only a few early cancellations due to bad weather. The major disappointment had been the failure to disembark nearly 300 passengers from visiting *MV Balmoral* in June - just when it had seemed like an almost perfect day.

With the departure of the crowds, Jenny and Chris were left to carry on work at the east end of the Barracks' roof. Their two-year repair programme is approaching completion but already further projects are being considered. During the Second World War the Barracks' south-facing windows were partially bricked in - presumably to resist attack damage. This means the wonderful view across Bridgwater Bay is obscured from the Barracks' long-room. But the Barracks is a listed building (and quite right too) so window replacements will have to be properly done. At the same time, it would be good to restore the Victorian doorways and get the whole group of military buildings back to how they looked in 1867. That's part of the dream anyway.

As well as the roofs, Chris and Jenny continued work on John Jiggins' pond, scrub clearance and path maintenance. Most mornings, they carry out a circuit of the island, and having such a continuous presence means the comings and goings of Steep Holm's wildlife are closely observed. October proved to be a busy month. Swallows and martins passed through in large numbers - *en passant* to the warm south. On the 11th Tony Parsons recorded seeing a snow bunting, a bird that breeds in the Arctic but overwinters in Britain, usually in mountainous regions like the Cairngorms. The bird has striking black-white plumage and was last seen on the island 30 years ago. On November 6th, hundreds of chaffinch passed over in flocks, taking up much of the day. As well as chaffinch, Chris and Jenny see greenfinch, goldfinch and goldcrests on most days, and even managed a triple sighting of a little owl between 17th October and November 3rd.

One morning, they disturbed 700 racing pigeons which had roosted in the island's small sycamore wood at its eastern end. They rose in a massive grey cloud above the beach with the resident peregrine falcons going mad with excitement and not knowing which way to turn! According to Chris, in all the confusion, the pigeons got clean away.

Laboratory Battery, looking to Brean Down

The sharp, clear winter air allows the islands to stand out in vivid relief, sometimes so clear and bright you feel you might reach out and hold them. In late afternoon, the yellow December light makes the sea and the mud-flats glow gold as the sun settles behind Brean Down. Surfaces reflect and refract every last ray of the dying day.

STEEP HOLM - APRIL 2004

As with last year, *MV Bristol Queen* has been unable to make the season's first few trips to Steep Holm. Problems with her harbouring at Knightstone have led to the cancellations and it's really frustrating! It means that many people will miss the flowering of the famous wild peony which puts on its brief (a week or so), glorious display of single magenta blooms in early May. Hopefully, the sailings will be on again very soon.

Despite the lack of a ferry, the island trust is fortunate in its wardens. Chris and Jenny have their own small boat: the venerable *Skylark*. She was a former ship's lifeboat, powered by an ancient diesel engine which can be reassuringly started (like my dad's Austin 16) with a handle if all else fails (my father specialised in dead batteries). On a warm, late April morning *Skylark* started briskly and, with the tide falling below the lowest part of the Knightstone jetty, we chugged out west. We had previously been hoping to make this trip earlier in the week but wind and rain had put a stop to that. Now the sun was shining, picking out the Worlebury hillside where a crane swung high over the new Rozel building which, to my mind, was beginning to look a little too big for its boots.

About a mile out, the sea made a gentle argumentative swell over the shallows of the South Patches, before settling back to an easy roll, Steep Holm sitting squarely on the horizon. We made good time and had to saunter around the island, waiting for the tide to drop further, so we could set down *Skylark* on the eastern pebble beach.

As we passed below the northern cliffs Jenny called out there was a seal following in *Skylark*s' wake. I spotted the grey head and almost immediately it was joined by another. Two seals and we hadn't even landed yet - that was amazing! They followed us for a while, disappearing as we rounded Rudder Rock, indistinguishable from the flitting shadows of the low flying gulls.

The pebble beach was bathed in sunshine and, on this morning, sheltered and warm. Beaching *Skylark* was straightforward; she eased over to an accommodating 30 degree tilt which simplified the unloading of 42 bags of sand and cement, packs of soft drinks and a box of Mars Bars. The cliffs above the beach glowed with saffron splashes of naturalised wallflowers and, as we walked up the zigzag path, their scent mixed with the spiciness of Steep Holm's boss plant: alexanders. The gulls were actively nesting; small excavations lined the pathway, some already occupied by a single egg. The usual number is two or three. At the top of the path, close to the priory excavations, we were greeted by a sparkling peacock butterfly - later on in the day I came upon a red admiral with tired and faded wings, presumably worn out by the stresses of overwintering or an early journey from the continent.

On their previous visits this year, Chris and Jenny had begun restoration work on a substantial outbuilding that adjoins the main Victorian barracks. The precise function of this brick-built 'shed' is unclear. It has a wide and high entrance in its west wall, with tall windows to the north and south. Too grand for a storage shed or a pump house it would seem. Perhaps it stabled the island's mules? Somehow it doesn't seem large enough for that. Another of those Steep Holm mysteries.

STEEP HOLM - JUNE 2004

How could we have picked such a day?! Steep Holm never lets us down! But, as we approached Knightstone, grey clouds were building from the north-west and splots of rain were already patterning the esplanade. Ages of dry weather and now this. But there was still hope - the sea was calm, our ferryboat *MV Bristol Queen* was waiting patiently by the jetty, and a good crowd of waterproofed travellers were piling aboard. So, despite the forbidding skies, we were, at least, going to get to Steep Holm.

The sea stayed quiet and well-behaved for the hour-long journey but along the Welsh coastline rain was falling heavily and, by the time we were mid-channel, a dark bank of cloud had obscured it completely. More cloud was massing from the north. The auguries were not good.

But it wasn't raining on us. Not a dot as we rounded Steep Holm's Rudder Rock and motored below the southern cliffs. And wasn't that a flick of sun on the Barracks' roof? Before long we were disembarking onto the pebble beach and it felt remarkably warm and comfortable. Jenny and Chris said there had been 20 minutes of rain about half an hour before we arrived - and that had been the first rainfall in nearly two months. And sure enough, as we ascended the zigzag path above the beach, the sun broke through.

By the time Rosie and I arrived at the Barracks' Visitor Centre chairs were set out on the south-facing terrace and their occupiers were remarking on how amazing it was to be sitting in hot sunshine while the rest of Somerset and the Welsh seaboard were wrapped in gloom. I just reflected that Steep Holm was always like this - for me anyway. How could I have doubted it? And then Rosie asked me if I had remembered my factor 300 sun-cream and I hadn't. Ye of little faith.

some weed gathered from his home pond for the one he had helped
Jenny and Chris establish on Steep Holm. After he had landed, it was
some time before he realised he had left it aboard *Bristol Queen*.
So his pondweed was now on its way to Penarth. There, what was
thought to be some offensive material for waste disposal was placed
in a Welsh rubbish bin - information that John mournfully received
when the ferry returned for the evening pick-up.

Many of the gull chicks were now fully airborne and confidently
taking off from land and sea. A few were still vulnerable emergent
nestlings, and the protective, hair-parting sorties of their parents
confirmed this. Looking down from the north cliffs (that face
Penarth and John Jiggins' pondweed), the sea was peppered with
young gulls. Above them wheeled a pair of peregrine falcons who,
like me, were receiving the attention of parent gulls. The peregrines
seemed unconcerned, languidly ignoring the aggressive fly-bys.
I've been told they hardly ever take young gulls, but later, under the
sycamores and just off the zigzag path, I came across two explosions
of feathers. Jenny said they were pigeon feathers, most likely a
tame racing bird, taken there and plucked by a peregrine before
being fed to the falcon's young.

The Farmhouse ruins

6.45am and the phone's ringing. It's Chris Maslen, the Steep Holm warden. "The trip's off Howard. It looks OK at the moment but there's a wind force 5 to 7, backing south-east, predicted later this afternoon, so we might not be able to get back." Tomorrow, severe storms are forecast, with wind speeds up 70mph. But today, it looked as though we had a 24 hour window in which we could get various supplies and building materials on to the island. But it's not to be. Just too risky. It's even more frustrating for Chris and fellow warden Jenny Smith; they've spent most of yesterday loading up their boat *Skylark*. And now, with the shortening days, the increasingly dodgy weather and the Bristol Channel's perverse tides, it's hard to know when they might return.

Mind you, there's little point in getting upset about it. Sailing on the Severn Sea is like that - possibly the most challenging in the British Isles. It affords respect. John Cabot, setting sail in *The Matthew* to discover America, had to hang around in the Channel for weeks before a fair wind carried him out into the Atlantic.

9.10am. Chris drops in to collect a scan of Steep Holm we are planning to use for a postcard. The sun's shining and it's almost warm. Barely a hint of wind. "It's going to be bloody perfect, isn't it?!" he groans. The season's last three visitor boat trips on *Bristol Queen*, all fully booked, had to be cancelled. That's upwards of 260 people who had to be booked in, and then

telephoned the evening before to be told the next day's trip is off and their money returned. A lot of work for Joan and Stan Rendell. And then often the weather turns out to be fine - so we know they'll be wondering what all the fuss was about. But, in nearly 30 years of running visits to the island, people have only been trapped into an overnight stay on one or two occasions I'm told they were quite jolly affairs. Although some of the reluctant lodgers were unwell from a surfeit of Mars Bars.

12.15pm. High thin cloud. Easy sunshine. Just a flicker of a breeze through the trees. I would have been sitting in front of the Barracks around now. Cheese and Marmite sandwiches, perhaps a glass of Chris's island-brewed ale and the entire West Somerset coast laid out before me. I cycled down the Weston promenade an hour or so ago. The air was crystal clear and Steep Holm stood out sharp and bright in the Channel.

4.30pm. Drop in on neighbours Hilary and Paul Cossham. It turns out they have spent the morning at Stolford (on the Somerset coast, due south of Steep Holm) and bought some grey mullet (it's now by the stove, floured, waiting for the frying pan) from mudhorse fisherman Brendan Sellick. "We could see Steep Holm very clearly - it's quite a different shape from the version we see from Weston. It was a beautiful morning." Hey-ho...

5.20pm. The time we would have been heading back to Knightstone. Cold, but a clear blue sky. Almost dead calm. Bloody perfect in fact.

THE WARDENS' STORY -
CHRIS MASLEN'S ANGLE

We awake with screams of alarm ringing in our ears.
A cacophony of noise, waxing and waning. The gulls are
being visited by a predator: a buzzard perhaps, or a
sparrow-hawk, or even a greater black-back gull - all on
the prowl for their breakfast. Who needs an alarm clock
with this daily occurrence?! The problem is, it takes place
at between 4.30 and 6.30 in the morning. Despite
turning over and pumping the pillows, the effort to get a
little more sleep bears little hope - the gulls are now fully
alert, busy bickering and back to making their usual
strident declarations over territory.

Muscles aching and twinging from the rigours of the
previous day's efforts, thoughts turn to the day ahead.
But nothing will happen until the first brew, followed by
the momentous decision of what to have for breakfast -
even though what's on offer is pretty limited. We mull
over this while washing or shaving. During the time the
domestics are taking place, the weather will have been
noted and plans for the day amended accordingly. There is
a splendid and ever-changing view of the Bristol Channel
from our kitchen window. The sea often turbid and
restless, sometimes smooth and glassy, at others a chaos
of white horses.

We can, accidentally, introduce more urgent work to
take precedence over the ongoing projects! For instance,
we had noticed a family of wrens which had taken up
residence in the east wing of our Victorian Barracks. The
parents had been dutifully flying in and out of the building
through convenient 'holes in the fabric' while bringing up
their young. So, when the time had come to fly the nest,
the parents led the way and popped out through a hole

over the top of a window. The youngsters couldn't quite understand that the hole was above the window and kept trying to go out through the glass. After a couple of days it became clear they were not going to make it and a helping hand was called for. The window was eased open and, since the wood was 'ripe' and the window hadn't been moved for at least 15 years, we took great care. With other work to attend to, we then disappeared.

Chris's hat

On our return, we discovered the window was even more rotten than we had thought and 90% of it had dropped eight feet to the ground. Amazingly, only one pane out of six had smashed, although its supporting frame had completely disintegrated. This was a mini-disaster, for the building was now open to the elements. On the mainland you could phone up 'a man with a van' to deliver some plywood to board up the offending hole. On Steep Holm this is not an option. Much of the time we have to make do and mend, and one has to be versatile and use whatever material we have to hand. All our other projects now had to be moved to the back burner, while we constructed a new window frame from recovered roof timber. This we then fitted and glazed with the five surviving panes of glass and one piece of board. A nice reward for trying to be helpful! As for the wrens - well, they're out there somewhere!

Continued

Most days, we patrol the island to see how things have fared and whether we have any visiting wildlife. Each day is different.

This year we had a runaway buzzard take up residence for a while. The gulls, as already mentioned, didn't take too kindly to its presence, but the buzzard didn't seem to mind being mobbed as it gracefully glided around the island. Unfortunately, this particular bird had clearly been raised in captivity and it didn't have the necessary skills for survival in the wild. We found it dead after two weeks of its solitary meanderings.

The Muntjac deer often bring down small avalanches of soil and rock onto the main path that zigzags from the East Beach to the perimeter path running round the top of the island. These falls have to be cleared before any visitors arrive, for the path's gradient is difficult enough without the need for scrambling over piles of spoil. Another hazard is the brambles which shoot out their sneaky, thorny stems almost overnight it seems and, swaying at eye level are, forever, a threat of mischief to the unwary. Nettles grow tall and, unable to support their large leaves, bend over into the paths ready to attack anyone in shorts. Our volunteer workers usually deal with these minor transgressions of nature on 'tripper days' while at the same time amiably dealing with numerous enquiries from island visitors as they pass by.

Whatever we do, the hours pass quickly and, as afternoon wears into evening, it's time to down tools, clean up, wind down and have a glass of island-brewed ale with something to eat. We'll need the rest, for we can be sure of one thing: tomorrow morning we shall be having an early call!

Jenny

With the visiting season due to start at the end of April, Chris and Jenny had several things to do to get the island ready. The main one was to deliver fifty one chairs (the island trust had bought them from Wells Cathedral) to the Victorian Barracks. Despite the crowd, Chris said there would be plenty of room on *Skylark* should I care to come along.

Yesterday, it had rained non-stop but today, although it was solidly overcast, there was no wind and even a prospect of sunshine in the late afternoon. An 11.5 metre tide was falling as I arrived at Knightstone, and *Skylark* was waiting by the jetty already loaded (I noted rather guiltily) with the Bishop of Bath and Wells' chairs, along with gas cylinders, drinking water, diesel and about a million bird and bat boxes! We waited until the tide fell level with the bottom of the jetty; this meant that by the time we arrived at Steep Holm, Chris would be able to beach *Skylark* without too long a wait before we could begin to unload. The passage across was uneventful, even though the high spring tides had scoured the Estuary's beaches of their flotsam and jetsam; so we had to watch out for the occasional wandering tree trunk.

We circled the island. The gulls were already marking out their nesting territory although Jenny didn't feel they had all arrived back after overwintering on the mainland. On the steep, northern cliffs a good number of cormorants were standing, black and dinner-jacketed, to attention - they are magnificent birds and it's hard to credit that the Department of the Environment issues licences for having them shot (in their thousands) by commercial fisheries! Even worse is the fact that the licence period includes the breeding season

when orphaned fledglings would die of starvation. We hope the DoE will think again.

After landing, we collected the trusty Honda load-carriers from the island top and began the long job of unloading the Bishop of Bath and Wells' chairs from *Skylark* onto the load-carriers, up the pebble beach, up onto the top of the quay, then back into the load-carriers and up the zigzag path to the Barracks. All this took a good few hours and it was 6 pm before the job was done. As forecast, the cloud-cover began to break up in the west, the sun showing through with bright shafts of yellow and gold light.

We were back on *Skylark* by 7.30pm, waiting for the sea to lift us from the pebble beach. From behind the dark island, the evening sunlight streamed out on either side, illuminating the lighthouse on Flat Holm and then the entire Somerset seaboard. The promontories of Clevedon, Sand Point, Worlebury and Brean Down glowed with extraordinary golden light, Brent Knoll and Crook's Peak joining in. All the windows of the buildings along the shoreline sparkled and flashed against the sombre backdrop of the night sky, which had the black intensity of a brooding storm. Then suddenly, with all this going on before us, two broad columns of rainbow light climbed out of Clevedon to the north and Burnham in the south. For a short time the huge rainbow completed itself above us, but mostly it was two, fantastic light shows going on simultaneously in widely separated seaside towns. As the sun set, the display gradually faded and *Skylark* began to stir, restlessly, on the pebbles.

A while later, a friend asked me if I had seen the wonderful sunset from Weston a few nights previously. Well I hadn't, not really; Steep Holm had blocked the view. But what I had seen was once in a lifetime stuff!

STEEP HOLM · MAY 2005

You may know Steep Holm's Kenneth Allsop Trust succeeded in getting a Heritage Lottery grant so it can complete the restoration of the island's Victorian Army Barracks: a Grade II listed building. Chris and Jenny have spent much of the past five years restoring the Barracks; now the Trust will be able to remove the Second World War bricks that partially block the south-facing windows, and put back sash windows to the original twelve pane design. For the first time since the war it'll be possible to sit inside the Barracks and enjoy the views out over Bridgwater Bay. The grant will also contribute towards replacing the tired, weather-beaten doors with new ones made from English oak, setting up an education area and improving the island's display presentation.* It's all very exciting.

Lackey moth caterpillar

I was lucky to hitch another ride on Chris and Jenny's good ship *Skylark* early in the month - on a day that looked as though it was going to be a bit choppy but which smoothed out very nicely in the end. Just as well, because there was a lot of heavy equipment on board; John Watts had donated a powerful bench drill (and its bench) which had to be got up to the Barracks' workshop on the island top. John, who was travelling with us, also hoped to sort out an alternator which was giving trouble. Also on board was Shane Coles who was planning to measure the doors and give the Trust a quotation for their replacement.

Before we landed, we skirted round the southern cliffs where Jenny pointed out a family of ravens, with three chicks, nesting on a high ledge. Ravens breed on Steep Holm fairly frequently, although I'd never seen them this clearly before. They are Britain's largest perching bird and regarded as creatures of ill-omen - something probably earned from their unpleasant habit of feeding on corpses left hanging on the gallows! Once on the island, Jenny also pointed out some beautiful, small, gold-winged moths with long flickering antennae *(Adela reamurella)* flying in and around the brambles - they looked like flittering fragments of gold-leaf. Unfortunately, I also have to report the return of the lackey moth caterpillar which ate everything in the rose family (bramble, whitebeam, hawthorn, strawberry plants etc.) on the island a few years ago. There was a report in the Weston Mercury they were also busy eating the town's cherry trees! We continue to be anxious about our precious wild peonies. In recent years they have been afflicted by a persistent fungal infection. I found a few in flower at the priory site, but they're going to need great care and protection.

Good news about the newly born seal that Jenny and Chris discovered abandoned on the pebble beach a few weeks ago. She's doing well and her seal-sanctuary carers have given her the name 'April'. There's every expectation she will eventually be able to return to the wild.

When *Skylark* motored off in the early evening, Shane had his door measurements and John had the faulty alternator stowed on board, as well as one of the Victorian doorway fanlights he was keen to repair. By the end of the year we won't recognise the old Barracks - but a passing Victorian gunner from the 12th Brigade, Royal Artillery just might.

*The new doors and fanlights were paid for with a grant from The Weston-super-Mare Trust.

Jenny with Grey seal pup 'April'

I seem to have acquired a reputation for being late. Now I would dispute this. I'm just not very good at being early. It was a perfect morning: the sea smooth, a soft, blue sky, a hint of a breeze. Plenty of time. I was striding easily along the Promenade and so was a little unnerved to see *MV Bristol Queen* looking as

Joan and Stan Rendell 'counting them aboard'

though she was about to head off. Come to think of it - why was there was no-one at the top of the steps ushering people aboard? Why no-one on the quayside casually chatting and playing with ropes? There was a definite feeling of imminent departure. All this on a perfect morning. So, even though I had arrived eight seconds early, there was *Bristol Queen* waiting to go, with querulous faces looking up as I hurried down the Knightstone jetty. I knew what they were thinking. They were thinking: "There's always one…" And I was actually eight seconds early! "7 ..6.. 5.." counted down Tony Parsons with his Mariner's Chronograph as I fell aboard. "Hello Howard" said Joan.

We made comfortable time across to the island; the early morning chill was gone and the sun was soon feeling warm on our faces. Steep Holm stood in a seemingly still sea, green and luxuriant, with a becoming blush of tree mallow covering the cliffs and the scree slopes all the way round the island. We seem to get a great flowering of this blowsy plant every few years, after which it retreats to a just a few battle-scarred veterans plotting the next campaign. After we landed, walking up the path from the beach, the entire area under the cliffs was chockful of purple-pink mallow, with solitary plants perched on outcrops above us. According to Rodney Legg and Tony Parsons, in their book *'Steep Holm Wildlife'*, tree mallow was first noted on the island in 1773 and probably had a medicinal role. It was used in ointments and poultices; an extract of the leaves was a treatment for sprains and the flowers were employed in the production of a dye.

The day turned hot, but despite this Dave Wallace and his Shirkers managed to lay the foundations to a new wall below the cliff path where masonry had collapsed. Above the South Landing, Andy Watkins was busy repointing the Victorian lime kiln where the stone-work had loosened. Andy had repaired the rain-water cistern under his Georgian house in Bristol, so he came with considerable experience in lime-putty mortars!

Leaving Knightstone

The coolest place on the island was in the shade of the sycamore wood. The trees grow on the eastern slopes above the pebble beach facing Weston, and the zigzag path wends its way though the wood to the top of the island. I was sitting on steps that lead up from the wood, when a burst of bird-song came from somewhere around me. I recognised it as a blackcap - I had last heard that wonderful sound in woodland near Watchet in West Somerset, when Rosie and I were searching for nightingales! I've yet to hear a nightingale, but for now I'll settle for a blackcap singing its heart out in Watchet or in Steep Holm's sycamore wood.

208 Steps

It was a
warm still day on the
island with low cloud and a
flat sea, the predicted sun never quite
managing to make an appearance. Below the
northern cliffs, the water was dotted with huge numbers of
young gulls: brown smudges on the brown sea, the surface
disturbed by the merest undulation. Effortlessly, the youngsters
were taking a trip on the tide-race; towed westwards as the sea
made one of its twice-daily departures from the Bristol Channel.
I was watching all this from the top of the 208 steps leading down
to a Second World War searchlight post that clings to the north
cliff-face, 20 metres above the sea. It was dry and there was no
wind so, with a healthy dose of apprehension, I made the descent,
wondering all the while how the Army had managed to build the
platform here in the first place. And it must have been a
desperate post to man on a stormy, winter night! In their book
'Steep Holm Pioneers', Stan and Joan Rendell describe war-time
blackout conditions in which several men were lost falling
over the edge.

The searchlight chamber's iron doors have long rusted away;
they lie in shattered fragments on the floor. The great, curved
metal shutters, which once protected the lights, became so
corroded they had to be removed - so many of the Second World

War constructions are falling to bits, while the Victorian buildings and gun batteries look as though they will last forever.

I once hid some money above the shutters' frame for my nephew Tom to discover and a treasure map to show the way. My brother told me Tom made the journey down the steps without a blink, but wasn't too impressed to find just a 50p piece of treasure. So I had to compensate with a monster bar of chocolate. And he certainly didn't notice the view - it takes in Flat Holm (where a sister light illuminated the Channel), the Welsh seaboard and nesting cormorants, the birds launching and swooping out over the sea. Steep Holm has one of the largest nesting colonies of cormorants in the South-West.

Meanwhile, down below, the young gulls were still bobbing about but now accompanied a large tree-trunk - a tree-trunk I hadn't noticed before which vanished and then reappeared with a whiskered nose and flippers. It was one of our grey seals making a languid materialisation. I turned away for a moment, and looking back he was gone. Later in the day I was to see two of them (I think) at the pebble beach; they were curiously inspecting another group of the island's visitors, line-fishing from the shingle spit - I hope the seals did better than the fishermen who only managed to catch a single conger eel. (But I'm pleased to report I was able to catch a monster slice of Pam Wallace's cake.)

Cormorants

When I re-emerged from climbing back up the 208 steps - partly on hands and knees and not looking down - I met Tony Parsons coming along the perimeter path. He showed me some intriguing, tiny bundles of grass stems, about one cm long, attached to the wall of the searchlight generator house. I would never have noticed them in a million years. They were the protective cases built by 'bag-worm' moth caterpillars and in which they pupate - the female moths are wingless and so they've been stuck on Steep Holm since the rise in sea levels 10,000 years ago! Island wardens Chris and Jenny will sympathise with that.

Having secured the Lottery Heritage grant for the restoration of the Victorian Army Barracks' windows and doors, we now had the problem of getting them made and installed. Amazingly, the doors seemed to be finished before they were ordered but, as always with an island in the middle of the Bristol Channel, delivery wasn't included. The doors and their frames are made of English oak and they are very heavy. Once again, Chris and Jenny and their boat *Skylark* were to demonstrate their versatility. On, as Chris described it, "a steamin' hot day" the doors were loaded onto *Skylark* which then set off on the morning tide.

Once the boat was berthed on the pebble beach, the Honda load-carriers were brought down from the workshop (formerly a generator house for one of the island's searchlights during the

Second World War) and the doors lowered onto them, one by one. The beach has quite a slope, so it's not easy to get to the foot of the quay as the carriers' caterpillar tracks skitter over the pebbles. Then there is the quay wall which rises another six metres above the beach. Here a winch has been installed so, painstakingly, the doors were cranked slowly up to the top of the quay. The day got hotter. "We always seem to pick steamin' hot days for this sort of thing!" said Chris. "We drank litres of water and we needed it!"

With the doors safely on the top of the quay, there was then the task of getting them to the top of the island. Once again the load-carriers proved invaluable and by judicious stacking the doors were able to negotiate the twisting path to the island summit. But by now the tide was coming in and *Skylark* would be twitching on her pebble berth. The doors were quickly secured in the workshop with the carriers, any longer and *Skylark* would have been off sailing alone. If only delivery had been included...

By the time I was on the island a few weeks later, the doors were safely in the Barracks. They looked beautiful, with that exquisite freshness in the grain of newly planed wood. But untreated wood wouldn't last long in Steep Holm's often hostile environment, so already some of the doors were on the bench being treated with a weather resistant stain.

A few weeks later again, I was back on *Skylark*, this time with a team of volunteers well qualified in carpentry to start on the installation of the doors. It was decided to begin with the big double set at the west end of the Barracks. These have a keystone above them with '1867' carved into it and they once led to the Master Gunners' quarters. It took all four of the team, which included Chris, to place and position the fanlight and the door frame - there was a moment when the doorway was filled with Roger and Roger, Pete and Chris, all holding spirit levels and various door-parts, as marks and adjustments were made. In the end, it went very smoothly and by the time we had to leave, the doors and the fanlight were handsomely in place. Meanwhile, in Weston, eight hardwood windows and their sash boxes are being made. Has anyone a spare helicopter?

It's been an exciting month on Steep Holm with over five years work on the Victorian Barracks' Visitor Centre suddenly coming together. At the end of August we had got the English oak doors onto the island and, one by one, they've been carefully fitted by Chris and some skilled volunteers, especially Roger Allsop. Then David Huish, who runs a joinery in Weston, announced that the island's order of eight sash windows (including their box frames) for the Barracks were ready!

On an early September morning the good ship *Skylark* was piled high with windows (with glass already puttied in), frames and weights, and we set off from Knightstone jetty in warm sunshine and a calm sea. Safely beached on Steep Holm's pebbled shore, it took three of us most of the day to unload the boat. One by one the window sections were lowered onto the load-carriers and transported up the steep incline of the beach to the high jetty where they were winched to the top of the quay. I seemed to spend quite a bit of time smoothing out my thumbprints which kept appearing in the soft putty - I think I got rid of them but there's bound to be residual evidence for a future forensic archaeologist. We got the window sections up to the Barracks, but had to leave the frames stacked on the quay so that we could get back to Weston on the incoming tide. Dave Wallace and his Shirkers would complete the transportation effort when they journeyed across on *Bristol Queen* the next day.

Two weeks later, three of us were accompanying Chris and Jenny back to the island on *Skylark* once again. During the intervening time David Huish had fitted the windows and they were, according to Chris; "looking great and working perfectly". I was dying to see them, and it was one of those moments when realisation exceeded anticipation. By removing the Second World War brickwork that had blocked out the lower half of the windows, and replacing each of them with two free-moving six-paned sashes (with putty thumb marks), the atmosphere of the of the Barracks' long-room had been completely transformed. Sunlight poured through the south-facing openings into what had been a rather gloomy and confining hall. Through the beautifully finished windows, I could look out over the terrace and Steep Holm's southern cliffs to the sparkling silver sea of Bridgwater Bay. Beyond were the soft Quantock hills and Dunkery Beacon, then Exmoor closing down on Porlock and onwards to Foreland Point.

A short while ago Jenny came across a small species of lobster (*'Axius stirhynchus'* - it has no English name) under a stone on the pebble beach. It'll never fit the pot for a Lobster Thermidor - it only grows to around three inches long. According to Tony Parsons, this particular crustacean, although quite common around Porlock, has not been recorded as far up-Channel as Steep Holm before. It's pink in colour and, like the common lobster, comes with a pair of unequal claws: one for crushing its prey, the other for snipping it up. Steep Holm continuously comes up with surprises - and you should see the windows.

2005 closed on a sad note with the death, in November, of John Fowles, the island's Trust President. John, one of Britain's outstanding literary talents of the 20th century, was a close friend of Kenneth Allsop, the campaigning environmental journalist, in whose memory the island trust was set up in 1974. Indeed John Fowles, along with John Percival, Rodney Legg and Betty Allsop (Kenneth's widow) were the prime movers in the formation of the Memorial Trust which finally managed to buy the island (which the owner, Mrs 'Ziki' Robertson, presented at a hugely reduced price) in March 1976. The conveyance was signed in the main room of John Fowles' home, Belmont House, in Lyme Regis. His support and enthusiasm sustained the Trust during its difficult early years and he was its Chairman until 1986. Trust Secretary Joan Rendell writes "For John, Steep Holm was a place of enchantment and he responded to its moods…" He even kept a bed of Steep Holm peonies (raised from seed) growing in his garden. Sadly, he didn't get to see the recent work that has so transformed the Victorian Barracks - he would have especially enjoyed the dazzling effect of sunlight pouring through the previously half-bricked windows.

I rarely get out to Steep Holm during the winter. As I previously described in this column a few years ago - in December 1989, Rosie and I were rounded up into a volunteer group to plant native trees along the island's more sheltered southern slopes. Only in December there's no such thing as a sheltered place on Steep Holm. We lit a desperate fire in the Barracks' hall; it looked pretty but didn't raise the temperature one degree, and Rosie reckoned she had never been so cold in all her life.

Sailings to the island will be rather sparse this year and the first trip won't be until May 27th - well after the flowering of the wild peony. It's also been impossible to arrange weekend trips during June and July; indeed July is reduced to a paltry two crossings. This is all down to boat availability and the tides - coping with the vagaries of the tide-table will always be a challenge to the boating programme. I had hoped to accompany Chris and Jenny on a building supplies trip in late April (Chris and Jenny have been back on the island since the beginning of the month) but the forecast of an evening Force 5 north-easterly forced its cancellation. Needless to say, the day turned out warm and sunny with scarcely a breath of wind and I had to be satisfied with looking out to the island from above Birnbeck Pier - beautiful in the clear air, and inaccessible.

With the dry spring weather, Chris and Jenny have been continuing work on the flat roof of the Barracks' East Block extremity which is going to be sealed with a new membrane. In Victorian times, this was the latrine house - unwisely sited close to the water tanks! The leaky roof has frustrated the completion of the East Block Education Area (part of the Heritage Lottery Award Scheme) - once it is sealed and the walls allowed to dry out, the area can be decorated and the cabinets and display boards installed.

STEEP HOLM - MAY 2006

The anticipated Saturday, May 27th sailing didn't happen. The whole week before had been cold, wet and windy with the entire country undergoing a January rerun. By Friday afternoon, it was clear the trip was going to be impossible - desperately disappointing for the ninety people booked for the crossing on Bristol Queen.

Two weeks earlier I had been luckier. Chris and Jenny had e-mailed me to say the weather and sea were at last behaving themselves, and they hoped to get a load of building materials over to the island. The morning turned out clear and bright, and above the Knightstone jetty the old baths and theatre buildings stood eviscerated and stark - we could see straight through the hollowed out arches of the pavilion to the hill behind. In a few years, Knightstone Island will be a changed place for the loss of the baths was a conundrum a variety of councils weren't prepared solve. But, despite many reservations, it's good to see a halt to the relentless deterioration of these much-loved buildings. Anyway, for the present, the view from Chris's boat *Skylark* was much the same - although the yacht club building was now missing.

The Inn

The sea was smooth and the journey an easy roll. As we approached, the island emerged from a light shrouding haze while the mainland retreated into an indistinct impression. The sun felt warm and there was a gentle southerly breeze. From the boat, we could see the bright splash of yellow wallflowers filling every cranny of the eastern cliffs. Above the pebble beach alarmed gulls wheeled, and there was a flash of white and black as shelducks took off from the lower crags of Tower Rock. *Skylark* crunched onto the pebbles and we waited as the sea retreated to leave us high and dry. The old inn still clung to the cliffs above the beach. Built in 1832 and believing itself to be outside Somerset's licensing jurisdiction; it had quite a reputation for carousing and smuggling during the mid-19th century. It wasn't until 1885 that the Inland Revenue spoilt things, whereupon landlord Fred Harris promptly moved over to Flat Holm - where his family did very well selling alcoholic beverages to the 'sabbath-dry' Welsh for another 40 years! The story's well told in Stan and Joan Rendell's book Steep Holm Pioneers.

Ascending the zigzag path through the sycamore wood, a blackcap was in full glorious voice. Later in the day I was to hear a whitethroat singing at the priory site and where, to my amazement, the wild peonies were in full flower - the cold March weather had stalled them by over two weeks. Up at the Barracks, Chris and Jenny showed me the newly installed 'cooler cabinet' purchased by Andrew and Joy Wilson so they'd no longer have to endure the novel Steep Holm experience of tepid gin and tonics. Jenny also told me that this year the cormorants were nesting in greater numbers and had invaded some of the gull sites higher up on the northern cliffs. Accompanying naturalist Tony Parsons on a reconnoitre of the island, this proved to be so with families of cormorants perched quite close to the perimeter path. The gulls didn't seem to mind - they were far too busy beating one another up. Quite a few broken gulls' eggs littered the path which Tony reckoned to be the result of raiding magpies or ravens.

Back at the beach, the island's resident grey seal dropped in for a visit; with his head poised magisterially above the waves, he appeared to be anticipating one of Andrew and Joy's cooler-cabinet cocktails.

Chris and Jenny had been up before 6am and launched their inflatable from the island. After a bouncy crossing, they arrived in Knightstone harbour on the rising tide, moored the inflatable, and positioned their boat Skylark on the harbour slipway to receive the internal shutters that would complete the work to the island's Barracks' windows. By the time I arrived, the shutters were on board and Skylark was parked alongside Bristol Queen waiting for the tide to fall.

It was an easy crossing and Steep Holm had taken on the soft purpling of tree mallow on the slopes above Rudder Rock and the southern cliffs. With Skylark driven onto the pebble beach, we waited awhile for the sea to retreat completely. While we waited, Jenny pointed out to me a female mallard with two tiny ducklings (minute balls of fluff) scurrying along the footings of Tower Rock. In no time they had made the sea and, to my astonishment, were negotiating the fearsome rip currents that make landing on Steep Holm so difficult. And they did very well. Somehow, and against the tide, they gained the north end of the beach and rested awhile on some high stones - remnants of the pre-Victorian harbour. By the time we had unloaded the shutters and got them onto the quay, mother mallard and her chicks appeared to be setting off again - this time to make the crossing to the Somerset mainland! It seemed incomprehensible to me; the ducklings' chances of surviving that five miles of water appeared negligible. And while we watched, the trio were being strafed by gulls for whom a duckling would be easy meat. But they paddled on. Until they became the tiniest dots on a great wide sea and were lost beyond the magnification of our binoculars. We wished them luck. They would need it.

Clouded Yellows

After weeks of hot dry weather, a few days earlier rain had fallen steadily for 36 hours - hard at night and then soft summer rain for a further day. Steep Holm seemed to be making a great sigh of relief and the walk up through the sycamore wood was accompanied by a familiar earthiness, and once again a blackcap was in full song. Six weeks earlier the island's alexanders had been in flower, scenting the air. Now they were busy setting seed - Tony Parsons reckons that the Steep Holm alexanders produce 22 tonnes of seed in a season! Pity they can't be turned into biofuel for the island's

Henbane

generators. Now the predominant scent was of privet: sweet and rather like lilac gone wrong. Along the paths, blue flowered clumps of iris accompanied splashes of ox-eye daisies, then a solitary tall-standing henbane,* and tucked here and there were occasional clusters of hedge woundwort with their spikes of sombre-red flowers. Hedge woundwort, as its name attests, was a powerful medieval remedy for wounds and injuries. Along with its close cousin, betony, it was often grown in monastery physic gardens - so it may well have been brought to Steep Holm by the island priory's monks.

Later in the afternoon, I spent an hour or two laying a treasure trail for my granddaughter Sarah. She's passionately involved with 'Famous Five' adventures, and what better place could be than Steep Holm for an adventure! "Here's hoping for jolly good weather during the summer hols!"

We left the island in the early evening and during the journey back to Weston we kept an eye open for the mallard and her young. We didn't see them - it's a big sea out there.

*Henbane: Another monastery garden escape and a potent source of the alkaloid atropine. Employed as a sedative in medieval times and, potentially, a deadly poison; Dr. Crippen used it to murder his wife.

Last month I mentioned I had set up a treasure trail on Steep Holm for my granddaughter Sarah - who, at the age of seven and three-quarters, is into 'Famous Five' adventures. She has watched 'Five on Kirrin Island' about a thousand times and is able to quote every fragment of dialogue. I had placed the map in a box (with an obligatory false bottom) and hidden it in the kitchen of Steep Holm's old inn. With clues, the map gave directions to a dungeon below the Victorian cannon on Summit Battery.

Sarah is almost beside herself when she discovers the map - she has no problem with the false bottom - that's only to be expected after all! There's a fever of clue-reading at the Barracks and we all march off with purposeful intent to look for the dungeon below the gun and a mysterious, pink pebble...

On the north-west part of the island, above the Cormorant Cliffs, we find the 'path beneath the elders' behind Summit Battery. During Victorian times, this site contained emplacements for two, seven ton cannons with their underground ammunition stores. The superb 19th century masonry was partly destroyed during the Second World War when concrete platforms, taking six inch naval guns, were constructed. The Victorian guns are still there: one on the perimeter path and the other, close to its original position, in its circular barbette with steps leading down into the ammunition magazine (the dungeon) close by.

This area of Steep Holm, with its steep slopes and cliffs down to the sea is a popular nesting place for gulls and cormorants. The young cormorants are well grown, but the gull chicks range in maturity from a few that can already fly, to fledglings just emerging from the nest. The parent gulls are still fiercely protective, but Sarah scarcely notices their low-flying swoops as she presses on in search of 'gold ingots'. A feverish search under the gun reveals nothing. Could all this end in disappointment?

"Perhaps those steps go somewhere?"

"You've got a point there Grandad! Come on!"
Sarah leaps up, hesitates, and then, torch in hand, tentatively descends the damp, gloomy staircase. This is spider territory.

"I've found it!" Sarah holds up a big pink pebble "It must be here somewhere."

Two weeks earlier, while I had been setting up the adventure, I told Jenny and Chris where I had hidden things. Actually, I was a bit worried the map would be found by visitors who came to the island before Sarah got there. So Jenny said she would hide it on the morning of our trip. I was quite sure 'the treasure' would be impossible for anyone to find without the map. But I had reckoned without the ubiquitous Tony Parsons, island naturalist and spider-hunter extraordinary. A week or so after I had departed, he'd arrived breathless at the island Barracks with Sarah's treasure in his hand and sought out Jenny and Chris.

"Look what I've found! Some idiot's been hiding stuff in the Summit Battery magazine!"

Well, Sarah found her treasure (which she didn't know had already been discovered) where it was supposed to be. It was 'real treasure' too - Queen Victoria pennies and King George Vth half-crowns, sixpences, and a 1988, 2p piece that had slipped in by accident, but which Sarah didn't notice anyway.

END-PIECE

Looking east towards Brean Down from the pebble beach

In late August, Rosie and I got out to the island, for what will probably turn out to be, the final time in 2006. A few days earlier the journey had looked very uncertain with high winds and stormy weather - one night had been a terrific cacophony of lightning and explosive thunder in Weston. I usually enjoy a good thunderstorm, but this one had really made me jump! When we reached Steep Holm, Jenny and Chris told us it had made them jump too. One thunderclap had been accompanied by a vivid blue flash and they had wondered if the Barracks itself had been struck - but it was too wild and dangerous to venture out and inspect. Next day revealed that the Summit Battery Searchlight Generator House had been hit. We saw for ourselves that a top corner of the building had been blown away with a jagged scorch-mark down the wall and across the ground near by.

Later on that day, John Watts introduced me to 'Big Bertha', a 1950's single cylinder, five horsepower diesel engine (made by R.A. Lister of Dursley, Gloucestershire) which he has housed in the refurbished storehouse at the east end of the Barracks. For many years, Bertha had dutifully served the village of Ebbesbourne Wake, near Salisbury, pumping its tap-water from a nearby well. Now she would be driving a generator to supply the Barracks with electricity. And she looked very comfortable there, with John looking fondly on, as she chuntered away in her new home. A museum piece in herself!

It's now late October and Chris and Jenny are still on the island. So far it's been mild but damp, with the last of the migrating swallows passing through some weeks ago. Although autumn appears to have barely touched the mainland, the leaves have already left the trees in the sycamore wood.

For me, a final *Skylark* trip had to be abandoned because of uncertain weather, and the narrowing window of available daylight makes a later journey unlikely. Even for Chris and Jenny in their speedy inflatable it's difficult. On a recent 'supply run' they hit a deep wave trough and the craft's bow submerged.

"The next thing I knew was the sea coming down my neck!" said Chris.

Anyway, it all means the display cabinets for the Barracks' Museum will remain flat-packed on the floor at Chris' and Jenny's home in Yatton until sometime in the new year. But there's always plenty to do on Steep Holm: new windows have been installed in the wardens' quarters along with internal shutters to the Barracks' north-facing windows. They've started work on the south side where fitting the shutters has proved to be fiddly, taking longer than expected. But Bertha is settling in well - so at least with winter closing in, the Barracks' lights will be on.

Howard Smith
October 2006

ACKNOWLEDGEMENTS

We should like to thank Laura and Allan Hoyano for their advice on the text. Joan and Stan Rendell and Tony Parsons have always been generous with their guidance and knowledge of the island. A special thank you to Chris Maslen and Jenny Smith for their kind hospitality and their reports of what was happening on Steep Holm. To a significant extent, this book is a record of their six years hard work. Their good ship *Skylark* deserves a mention here too!

Once again, thanks to David Brown for his support, and to our designer Colin Baker who has again pulled our ideas together into a coherent whole.

Thanks also to Judi Kisiel, editor of the *Weston and Somerset Mercury,* who, through features, and the articles upon which this book is based, has succeeded in getting Steep Holm so much better known on the mainland.

A BIBLIOGRAPHY OF STEEP HOLM

Barrett, J.H. 1993, A History of Maritime Forts in the Bristol Channel.

Kenneth Allsop Memorial Trust & Fowles, John, 1978, Steep Holm - a case history in the study of evolution.

Knight, F.A. 1902, The Sea-Board of Mendip.

Legg, Rodney, 1985, The Steep Holm Guide.

Legg, Rodney and Parsons, Tony, 1990, Steep Holm Wildlife.

Legg, Rodney, 1991, Steep Holm at War.

Legg, Rodney, 1992, Steep Holm, Allsop Island.

Legg, Rodney, 1993, Steep Holm, Legends and History.

Rendell, Stan and Joan, 1993, Steep Holm - The Story of a Small Island.

Rendell, Stan and Joan, 2002, Steep Holm - The Trail Guide.

Rendell, Stan and Joan, 2003, Steep Holm's Pioneers.

Worrall, D.H. and Surtees, P.R. 1984, Flat Holm.

The Steep Holm Map is based on an original by Malcolm Noyes.